Are You Happy @ Work?

Are You Happy @ Work?

**Identify Your 'Happiness Factors' -
Attempt H.I. [Happiness Inventory]**

Dr. Yogesh Pahuja

PARTRIDGE
A Penguin Random House Company

To order additional copies of this book, contact
Partridge India
000 800 10062 62
orders.india@partridgepublishing.com

www.partridgepublishing.com/india

CONTENTS

PREFACE

This book is a result of 6 years of research. I started to work on 'happiness at work place' in 2008 and soon the research evolved into development of Happiness Inventory [H.i].

During my doctoral work, I personally administered tools to over 800 employees for developing this inventory. This journey was highly enriching and gave me insights into 'what made people happy or unhappy at work place?'. As a matter of fact after administering the tool I often ended up discussing with the employees and HR managers several facets that went into creating a happy environment at work place and how a happy employee makes a difference in productivity.

I was awarded doctorate on my thesis, which primarily showcased Happiness inventory [H.i] with 180 factors. The next day when I woke up, it dawned upon me that my journey to spread happiness has actually just begun. I made it a point to further my research and started working on my Inventory and as a part of my post doctoral work & evolved the final cluster based 164-factor inventory with a Cronbach alpha of

0.88 to 0.94 indicating a very high level of internal reliability of the tool.

In order to continue my mission of spreading happiness and taking my research to the masses, I decided to create a Mascot of Happiness. 'Dr. ChooHa' is a result of that thought process who now is an icon of my 'Happiness Studio' and joins me in reaching out to give away 'Smiley Awards' and 'Appreciation with a Smile'.

This book is the next logical happy step in spreading happiness as a choice. If you choose to be happy, you will be happy. It's that simple.

Your feedback and comments are welcome. Feel free to write to me at yogesh.pahuja@gmail.com and visit www.choosehappiness.in to know more.

Choose Happiness...Be Happy.

ACKNOWLEDGEMENTS

At the outset I would like to acknowledge my PhD Guide **Dr.D.M.Pestonjee** (retd. Prof. of IIM Ahmedabad) who is a true source of inspiration and a role model for all my academic pursuits. It was in a discussion with him that the idea of 'happiness' as a research area was born.

The contributions, support and learning from **Dr.S.M.Khan** who also helped me during my doctoral and postdoctoral work deserve a special mention here. He continues to be a source of inspiration. His approach to using statistics as a tool for research is simply incredible.

I must acknowledge my dear friend and graphic designer **Jignesh Parmar** (jiganesh82@gmail.com) who brought 'Dr. ChooHa' to life. His contribution is indeed noteworthy.

I also acknowledge all my **clients, respondents and organizations** who have supported me in some way or the other to complete the development of the Inventory, enriched my experience as a Trainer and OD expert. Special thank you for sharing their 'happy' experiences.

In the process of development of this book as a final version, it would be incomplete if I did not acknowledge the efforts of my professional colleagues **Gaurang Patel** and **Surabhi Poduval** who spent hours on it for editing and structuring.

I dedicate this book to my Parents **Dr.O.P.Pahuja and Mrs. P.L.Pahuja** who have shown me the true meaning of happiness and it is only with their direction and blessings I have reached here today. Their encouragement and support in my academic and professional pursuits is priceless.

And last but not the least I would like to thank my lovely wife **Nilam,** for being a true support and believing in me.

MEET THE MASCOT OF HAPPINESS STUDIO

Choose Happiness

Dr. ChooHa is an iconic representation of a messenger of happiness. The name is coined from two words '**Choo**se **Ha**ppiness'. A messenger that shows you the way to make your life joyful and happy. Dr. ChooHa believes that being happy is a matter of choice. If we choose to be happy, we will be happy and by choosing happiness we take the ownership individually to remain happy and spread happiness around us.

As a Mascot of 'Happiness Studio' [www.choosehappiness.in] Dr. ChooHa adorns several avatar, some of which you will discover in this book as you read along and on our web site from time to time.

Dr. ChooHA does not discriminate with color; caste, religion, gender, age or any other form. Dr. ChooHa is merely a symbolic human icon with one distinct characteristic and that is a smile – A smile that rubs off on you. This signature pose tells you to 'Keep Smiling' and 'Be happy'.

1

Building a perspective on happiness

Why Happiness?

Happiness as a subject has been the most researched and most sought after subject. It is until recently that people have started identifying that happiness is one of the key factors for the well being of an individual.

One of the pillars of positive psychology and commonly referred as subjective well being, happiness is as basic and elementary as drinking water or even breathing.

Several authors have worked upon happiness as a concept and most have spoken about it from the spiritual angle. The most commonly conveyed views include be patient, be blissful, meditate, always respond and not react to a situation and several other do's and don'ts. However it always raised a question in my mind. What is the reason of our happiness or unhappiness? Is it possible to find out why we are happy in one situation and why we are unhappy in another? So is happiness a state of mind or can we really quantify it? Is happiness restricted to only individuals or can a family or a social unit also be happy / unhappy? Can organizations be a happy place to work?

With several questions in my mind, I embarked on my research and took it up as my doctoral work in 2008. During this journey I personally went through several experiences on personal, family and professional front. All of these experiences taught me only one thing and that when we search a lot for happiness, we don't find it and that makes us unhappy. When we settle down to accepting the facts of life, adapt to the environment, become aware of our current status, decide to learn from it and move on, we suddenly discover happiness. In this book I have attempted to address some of these issues.

Prince Siddhartha ventured out leaving his luxury life behind in search for truth. The truth about why is there so much sadness in this world. As Lord Buddha, he gave to the world what we know as Vipassana.

Vipassana, which means to see things as they really are, is one of India's most ancient techniques of meditation. It was rediscovered by Buddha more than 2500 years ago and was taught by him as a universal remedy for universal ills and the resultant happiness of full liberation.

Thus, the pursuit of happiness is not new. It was recently in 1997 when Dr. Martin Seligman started his research on positive psychology where in subjective well-being (happiness) was seen as one of the pillars of positive psychology. It is around this time that a structured application oriented approach was being adapted for research on happiness.

In fact there is a World Database of Happiness that maintains an archive of research findings on subjective enjoyment of life called happiness since 1975 and is initiated by Ruut Veenhoven, Erasmus University Rotterdam & Happiness Economics Research Organization.

<u>Defining Happiness</u>

There are multiple definitions of happiness
that exist. Some of my favorites are:

"HAPPINESS equals REALITY
minus EXPECTATIONS"

"Happiness is an emotional state of well being characterized
by positive feelings ranging from contentment to intense joy."

"Happiness is a state of positive acceptance of current status
of our environment with a willingness to move on."

"Happiness is a journey called life."

"1st level is satisfaction, 2nd level is pleasure.
Happiness is a level beyond."

"A well guarded thought from within is
the bearer of true happiness."

"Happiness is a choice. Choose Happiness & be happy."

"Being Happy is easy. You simply have to be happy."

"Happiness is a state of mind triggered by right emotions."

<u>Where does happiness exist?</u>

I believe that one of the most important factors in life for each one of us is to be happy and joyful to really feel good. But when you are stressed out / unhappy it's like you have turned off your mobile and either the call doesn't ring or when the call comes in you can't hear it but for the ring tone in your own heart and mind.

No matter what happens life is precious and you should just "Be Happy" and have a great life.

It is therefore imperative to mention here about Bhutan and their model of Gross National Happiness.

- The remote Himalayan kingdom of Bhutan is the only country in the world, which puts happiness at the heart of government policy.
- Bhutan has even banned plastic bags and tobacco on the grounds that they make the country less happy.
- The one set of traffic lights Bhutan ever had was on a single junction. But people found it frustrating; so they went back to a human being to manage traffic.
- Buddhist prayer flags flutter in the wind. In Bhutan the government puts inner spiritual development on par with material improvement.
- One of the pillars of Bhutan's happiness philosophy is care for the environment. Strict conservation laws are aimed at achieving sustainable development.
- The capital, Thimpu, is remarkable for its lack of advertising. In an attempt to hold back consumerism the city council recently banned hoardings promoting Coke and Pepsi.

- Bhutan was the last nation in the world to introduce television in 1999. Recently they banned a number of channels including International wrestling and MTV, which they felt did little to promote happiness.

So one of the points that come to mind is how much of research has been carried out on happiness in the world. Well one set of world happiness statistics indicate:

- Over 9000 publications in Bibliography of happiness, of which 4500+ report an empirical study that is eligible for inclusion in the findings archive.
- 1000+ measures of happiness, mostly single survey questions varying in wording and response scale.
- 9000+ distributional findings in the general public across 150+ nations and 1900+ studies.
- 13000+ correlational findings observed in 1700+ studies, excerpted from 1300+ publications.

Now that is a lot of work to ensure smiles around the world. And this is just the beginning.

Happiness @ Work

❖ **The million-dollar question: Can Happiness Boost Employee Productivity?**

Happy Employees= Hefty Profits.

There's plenty of hard evidence that shows that happy employees lead directly to better performance and higher profits.

- Delaney launched HiHR **in 2009 and the company has made it to the Hawaii Best Places to Work list in every year for which it was eligible – four times straight now.** In the same time, HiHR went from revenues of $6.1 million in 2009 to $123 million in 2013.

- Consider Marriott, which offers employee discounts at its thousands of hotels worldwide. Work there 25 years, and you get free stays at the company's hotels and timeshares. Marriott has gained an average 11.3% a year for the past decade, vs. 7.9% for the Standard & Poor's 500-stock index with dividends reinvested.

- A review recently conducted for Britain's Department for Business Innovation and Skills (BIS) shows that employers can improve employees' wellbeing through improvements in job quality (Bryson et al. 2014).

- A 2012 Gallup meta-analysis of 263 research studies conducted across nearly 200 companies revealed that highly engaged employees translates into significantly more dollar signs—22 percent more, roughly. The $Q^{12®}$ report, titled **"Relationship Between Engagement at Work and Organizational Outcomes," found a 0.42 correlation between engagement and performance. Organizations whose employees ranked in the top half for employee engagement were almost twice as successful, and those in the 99th percentile showed quadruple the success rate over those scoring in the 1st percentile.**

The research still goes on. All studies have indicated a positive correlation with happiness and productivity. The happier the employees, chances are more productive they will be.

It's human to believe that success will bring you happiness. As a matter of fact research has proved that happiness is a precursor to success. Success doesn't make you happy so much as happiness makes you more successful.

Happiness @ work equation

More satisfied employees => happier employees => more engaged employees => more productive employees => a mutually beneficial equation for everyone.

It's that logically simple, really.
Also

A happy employee = A satisfied employee.
A satisfied employee = or ≠ A happy employee.

About Happy Work Places

New research confirms what Google already knows— *greater employee happiness results in higher productivity without sacrificing quality.*

The findings, published in the *Journal of Labour Economics*, included four different experiments with more than 700 participants.

During the experiments a number of the participants were either shown a comedy movie clip or treated to free chocolate, drinks, and fruit. Others were questioned about recent family tragedies, such as bereavements, to assess whether lower levels of happiness were later associated with lower levels of productivity.

Google has invested more in employee support and employee satisfaction has risen as a result. For Google, it rose by 37 percent.

Research has shown that happier subjects are more productive and the same pattern appears in different experiments. Such a research provides us a guideline for management in all kinds of organizations and that they should strive to make their workplaces emotionally healthy for their workforce.

The Search and Re-search for Happiness

In our society, the focused quest for material gain as conventionally measured typically makes lot of sense. Higher household income generally signifies an improvement in the life conditions.

Higher average incomes do not necessarily improve average well-being. The household incomes may have risen in the past whereas measures of average happiness have remained essentially unchanged.

The paradox is that at any particular time richer individuals are happier than poorer ones, but over time the society did not become happier as it became richer.

One basic reason is that we compare ourselves to others. We are happier when we are higher on the social (or income) ladder. Yet when everybody rises together, relative status remains unchanged.

While higher income may raise happiness to some extent, the quest for higher income may actually reduce one's happiness. In other words, it may be nice to have more money but not so nice to crave it.

In the same way it applies to happiness too. Craving for happiness as a matter of fact becomes a reason for unhappiness. Further, there is an exploitation of the belief (read myth) that you become happier by becoming richer.

What Next?

The journey to happiness at work begins with discovering the reasons that make you happy or unhappy. Once you identify the reasons / factors it becomes possible to make amendments in the way we work or approach situations at work. Honestly it's only a matter of making choices in our life. At every stage we will be faced with several situations. More often we tend to choose the easier way out knowing very well that it give us momentary relief or pleasure but we tend to consciously prefer not to take the hard way out in the interest of long term relief.

The first step to identifying your factors is through the **3D-model of happiness** evolved through research and is explained in the next chapter with real time examples that most of us will identify with.

2

Identify your Happiness Factors

So far we have tried to understand 'what is Happiness?' Now let us try to understand what **3D model of Happiness** is. As evolved from my research, the core happiness of an individual at work place lies in three dimensions; namely Individual, Organizational & Family / Social. Under each dimension there are clusters that contain sub factors of happiness or unhappiness at work place.

3D-Model of Happiness

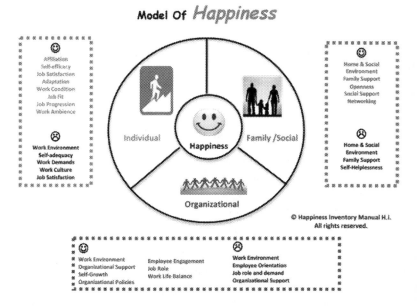

The three dimensions get further divided into Happiness & Unhappiness, thus making it six dimensions name Individual happiness & Individual unhappiness, Organizational Happiness & Organizational Unhappiness and Family / Social Happiness & Family/Social Unhappiness. Let us try to understand all 6 dimensions.

Dimension 1: Individual Happiness

Individual Happiness dimension includes clusters like affiliation, self-efficacy, job-satisfaction, adaptation, work condition, job fit, job progression and work ambience.

Affiliation

Affiliation indicates the extent to which you feel connection/ association with your organization in which you work.

Affiliation's sub factors are system & process, Vision Clarity, Boss & Seniors, Brand Name, Trust on team & Organization, Management support & Work Timings.

Some of the real time experiences shared by respondents, which highlight the examples of affiliation cluster, are as follows:

Please Note: All quotes have been reproduced with written consent of the respondent and have been edited for grammatical errors only. Their names and names of the organization are as per their preference to be quoted.

☺Happy Experience☺Affiliation☺HEIHAF01

"My job starts at 9 and but when it strikes 8.15 I get very excited due to my comfort on the job as there are different new things happening daily in our office, the amount of information I am able to grasp from my colleagues as well as my staffs which was not there in my previous job"

Name: **Organization:**
Hasanabbas N Momin **Retail Supermarket**

☺Happy Experience☺Affiliation☺HEIHAF02

"I feel connected to my organization, as I am given the authority in more than many ways. It builds an 'entrepreneur' in you. You can decide what is good or bad for the organization. Decide in more than many ways to negotiate with the client for a candidate, place the candidate. The sense of freedom given to me as an employee, lets me explore my skills, connects me to the culture of organization thus enhancing my potential"

Name: **Organization:**
Sarita Bhatt   **HR consulting firm**

☺Happy Experience☺Affiliation☺HEIHAF03

"Every day is a learning day as I am able to gain new knowledge about new technology of textile industry and it increases my experience to the next level which incites me to go to work and eagerly reach at my work place."

Name: **Organization:**
Arunan Poduval   **Textile Industry**

Self – efficacy

Self-efficacy explains your belief in your own ability to complete tasks and work allotted to you.

Self-Efficacy's sub factors are Skills, Dedication & Sincerity, Positive attitude, Learning attitude, Job profile Clarity, Performance & Job Security.

Some of the real time experiences shared by respondents, which highlight the examples of this cluster, are as follows:

☺Happy Experience☺Self-Efficacy☺HEIHSE01

"When I was in my masters I was not able talk confidently in front of people but now I can give live seminar in front of more than 200 people and feel confident"

Name: **Organization:**
Shailesh Chaudhari **Academics**

☺Happy Experience☺Self-Efficacy☺HEIHSE02

"I know my ability is relevant for this job as any problem that occurs such as any computer or machinery breakdown leads me to do that job effectively, and I feel very happy to rectify it as I am the only one who can fix it"

Name: **Organization:**
Hasanabbas N Momin **Retail Supermarket**

☺Happy Experience☺Self-Efficacy☺HEIHSE03

"As I graduated from an economics background I have a firm grip on economics. Hence being an economics professor has helped me to improvise my knowledge and share a great deal of knowledge with my students. Hence it allows me to complete any project or any assignment and also I am able clarify any doubts of my students"

Name: Pinky **Organization:**
(name changed) **Academics**

☺Happy Experience☺Self-Efficacy☺HEIHSE04

"I have different methods of teaching and my students were eager to accept the change in the teaching method as they were bored of the monotonous atmosphere. It allowed me to show my caliber where I got a perfect platform to showcase my innovative ideas forward. This made me satisfied and happy"

Name: **Organization:**
Surabhi Poduval   **Academics**

☺Happy Experience☺Self-Efficacy☺HEIHSE06

"One of our client wanted candidates with lots of option, initially he rejected 3 CVs from the first lot and changed the package and little bit JD also, then it was more difficult to find such candidates, but I was confident that I will search out anyhow. And after some efforts 3 candidates got shortlisted for final round out of 14 candidates sent to the client"

Name: **Organization:**
Tamanna (name changed)   **HR consulting firm**

☺Happy Experience☺Self-Efficacy☺HEIHSE07

"I joined here around 3 weeks ago. I came up with the execution plan to reach the goals; I am quite sure about myself that I can easily reach the goals with my skills. For example: I had to get 10 sign ups in 20 days. I contacted every client and explained about our services. some of them got excited about it and with my skill and belief I completed the task"

Name: VaibhavJayantibhai   Organization:
Solanki   **e-Business, IT Firm**

Job Satisfaction

Job satisfaction indicates your contentment with different facets of your job. Apart from salary and incentives, freedom, time management etc. explains job satisfaction.

Job satisfaction sub factors include Job Profile, Salary, and Independence in work, time management, Incentives.

Some of the real time experiences shared by respondents, which highlight the examples of this cluster, are as follows:

☺Happy Experience☺Job Satisfaction☺HEIHJS01

"Dealing with audience which is a mix of confident and not so confident, intelligent and not so intelligent, serious (about career) and easy going is not easy. At the end of the session, when you see that 'value addition' expression on almost every face and you know that time is constructively spent. A day starting with a 'wow' class is a day worth lived"

Name: **Organization:**
Ranna Vaishnav   **Academics**

☺Happy Experience☺Job Satisfaction☺HEIHJS02

"In my job profile I am able to get results quickly which is why I am enjoying my work. Whereas in my previous job I got frustrated with the amount of pressure I have to put on other employees to get things done, hence now at present I am satisfied with this job."

Name: **Organization:**
Arunan Poduval   **Textile Industry**

☺Happy Experience☺Job Satisfaction☺HEIHJS03

"I like to work in flexi job timing because in India there are lots of social responsibilities on everybody's shoulder, so very hard to maintain given task in given schedule. But this organization gives space in timing and also this organization allows me to give suggestion for better progress and changes. So whenever suggestion is appreciated I become happy."

Name: **Organization:**
Ruchir Mehta   **e-business, IT industry**

☺Happy Experience☺Job Satisfaction☺HEIHJS04

"I am good at designing. I am the only qualified person in my department who can understand and complete the job effectively and due to my experience I am able to guide my son as well. He has become a successful architect. That is why I am so much connected with my job"

Name: **Organization:**
R H Vyas   **Government office**

☺Happy Experience☺Adaptation☺HEIHA05

"I am an undergraduate so I have to adjust myself in every job. I have done different types of job. I am happy at transportation job. It is great time in my job because I am able to develop myself to handle all situations with all positive thoughts at work place"

Name: **Organization:**
Trivedi Naimish   **HR consultancy firm**

Work condition

Work condition signifies positive things about your workplace, which motivates you to go to work. It includes factors like location of office; distance from your home, support from your colleagues and self-motivation plays a role determining your willingness to go to work.

Some of the real time experiences shared by respondents, which highlight the examples of this cluster, are as follows:

☺Happy Experience☺Work Conditions☺HEIHWC01

"I started this job over here before 6 months ago just because I had passed through some personal problem in my life which made me alone but over here in my job all members help me to overcome that situation and make me so positive about life and its situations. Now I feel very positive about my life"

Name: **Organization:**
Hiren Sakarval   **Service Firm**

☺Happy Experience☺Work Conditions☺HEIHWC02

"I am always achieving my targets as I am getting the targets which motivate me to break my own records/ milestone. I always take targets as a challenge and try to fulfill that and at the end of the day that makes me happy that I am delivering what my company is expecting out of me"

Name: **Organization:**
Vibhuti Kiri   **Service Organization**

☺Happy Experience☺Work Conditions☺HEIHWC03

"whenever our assignment is over and candidate is placed by us in any organization it gives me motivation even if the assignment is tougher. I get to learn more things from our seniors and that too with positive attitude and motivation to work towards the goal"

Name: Shruti   **Organization:**
(name changed)   **HR consultancy firm**

☺Happy Experience☺Work Conditions☺HEIHWC04

"The staffs are very friendly, we work together, talk to each other, help out each other and go beyond our profiles which make us feel at home. Even the directors of the company helps us in our work, they speak to us as they are speaking to a friend. This atmosphere makes us feel comfortable and motivated to go to work"

Name: Vaibhav   **Organization:**
Jayantibhai Solanki   **e business, IT industry**

☺Happy Experience☺Work Conditions☺HEIHWC05

"I am very positive about few things at my work place which makes me motivated. Example- here we are getting space for any kind of implementation in the system. We have space of thinking which motivates us to create very good ideas, which can help organization in revenue and branding"

Name: **Organization:**
Kavya Basantani   **Academics**

☺Happy Experience☺Work Conditions☺HEIHWC06

"Even in my dreams I have not imagined that I will do my article-ship in such a big and well organized organization. Office area is structured in such a way that every person get enough space/ area to work and so we work in a very comfortable manner. Every day we have to face a new challenge which ultimately boosts up our thinking power and helps in understanding 'Bare Act'."

Name: Krushit Kaushikbhai Shah

Organization: Finance Sector

☺Happy Experience☺Work Conditions☺HEIHWC07

"Positive thing about my work place is my team leader. We don't have mental pressure and tension related to work. She always helps whenever required. Also not very stubborn related to office hours also (as it is very important for me as I have a small kid at home). Timings are very flexible and positive attitude of her makes me happy at work place."

Name: Shraddha (name changed)

Organization: HR consultancy firm

☺Happy Experience☺Work Conditions☺HEIHWC08

"The systematic flow of work motivates me to go. Here the system is good. The works done by my colleagues are good. The timings are flexible and there are no such restrictions as well as no work pressure here. The work goes through one to one procedure. I would like to work here only and this satisfies me."

Name: Meena (name changed)

Organization: HR consultancy firm

Job fit

How suitable are you for the current job is determined by your job profile, your nature, and your personality & job knowledge.

Some of the real time experiences shared by respondents, which highlight the examples of this cluster, are as follows:

☺Happy Experience☺Job Fit☺HEIHJF01

"I am better with accounting and since after the finance manager I am the one who they will approach for any auditing purpose, so I am fit for this job as I am able to provide better job output."

Name: **Organization:**
Suthar Qurbanhusain A   Retail Supermarket

☺Happy Experience☺Job Fit☺HEIHJF02

"it was bit difficult for me to find a job which would be suitable for me in terms of flexibility in time, work and leave which was resolved when I met sir and discussed my problems relating time as I have a small kid of 2 years for which sir gave me flexible time as well as allowed me to continue my studies with my job i.e. CS final exam. For me sir gives me the best options plus also shares his knowledge so that his employees can grow."

Name: **Organization:**
Zalak Jainish Shah   Finance Sector

☺Happy Experience☺Job Fit☺HEIHJF03

"I found my core area-finance in which I always wanted to work. And due to the freedom for work and time given by the management, it suits me and I am able to explore more in our ideas"

Name: Neha　　　　　　**Organization:**
(name changed)　　　　　**Retail Supermarket**

Job progression

What contributions your job is making in building your career is indicated through job progression. It includes factors like self-confidence, learning attitudes, tasks and challenges at workplace and growth opportunities.

Job Progression sub factors are learning opportunities & Challenges, Growth Opportunities, Taking Challenges.

Some of the real time experiences shared by respondents, which highlight the examples of this cluster, are as follows:

☺Happy Experience☺Job Progression☺HEIHJP01

"I am happy that my current organization could notice my potential which my former organization could not in 18 years. My current organization offered me ample opportunity to grow, learn and contribute. It has taken care of my progress by giving me four promotions in eight years. My job enabled me to interact with international leaders and travel internationally. I was given an opportunity to start, run and establish an entire institute when I was at the junior most position. In spite of challenges I have faced, my job has given me more than what I had expected"

Name:　　　　　　　　**Organization:**
Prof. (Dr.) Nigam Dave　**Academics**

☺Happy Experience☺Job Progression☺HEIHJP02

"For CA student like me, article-ship is very compulsory. During the article-ship tenure we deal with various problems which are related to my profession. Whenever I start my own practice, practical approach which I got from my article-ship period will help me a lot. So my present article-ship contributes a lot in building my career"

Name: Krushit　　　　**Organization:**
Kaushikbhai Shah　　　**Finance Sector**

☺Happy Experience☺Job Progression☺HEIHJP03

"This organization has given me good platform to enhance my career. I have done HR but my previous job did not contain anything about HR profile. After joining here I learned stepping stone to HR i.e. recruitment. I talk to people, understand their profiles, role, packages and this gives me a lot of knowledge to build my future in HR"

Name:　　　　　　　　**Organization:**
Kaushikbhai Shah　　　**HR consultancy firm**

☺Happy Experience☺Job Progression☺HEIHJP04

"I am career oriented. My one plus point is that I am a good recruiter because I am an HR person. Currently I am in consultancy so as per my view I got lot of knowledge about various portals, how to conduct interviews, how to define key words and many more things. So it is the best way to enhance my career"

Name:　　　　　　　　**Organization:**
Pooja K Panchal　　　**HR consultancy firm**

☺Happy Experience☺Job Progression☺HEIHJP05

"Its been only three months of joining this company but sir gave equal opportunity to everyone plus in three months I have learnt all types of work related to CA as well as CS which was my goal of life, which is achieved in short duration of time i.e. 3 months. Level of knowledge has increased and work efficiency is improved altogether. Sir is supportive in teaching work which is not very easy on other firms"

Name: **Organization:**
Zalak Jainish Shah   **Finance Sector**

☺Happy Experience☺Job Progression☺HEIHJP06

"My Company is ever growing. We have made remarkable progress in previous 2 years, where my immediate boss had resigned (2 times it had happened). I was asked to take over the whole responsibility. I was glad about the faith shown by them. Personally I am happy on my progress of handling things independently"

Name: **Organization:**
Gaurav Vesasi   **Manufacturing Sector**

☺Happy Experience☺Job Progression☺HEIHJP07

"It has been two years since I am in this current profile and in 2 years I have connected deeply with the profile. For example, while handling very regular position, where my skills are pretty limited, but the opportunity given to take over PAN India, gave me an edge in assessing candidates from various cities, interact with clients, understand the organizational culture, the fit ID and then speak to the right fit. This has in a way helped my personality, to be more astute in my judgments. Made me more career conscious and knowledge absorption in the process has made me a person who can contribute in locating right talent. All in all, a journey from being just a recruiter to identifying professionals and building their career"

Name: **Organization:**
Sarita Bhat   **HR Consultancy Firm**

Work ambience

Work ambience suggests the work environment of your job. It includes not only infrastructure but also facilities and appreciation/reward you receive from your work environment.

Work Ambience sub factors are Appreciation, Facilities & Work Environment. Some of the real time experiences shared by respondents, which highlight the examples of this cluster, are as follows:

☺Happy Experience☺Work Ambience☺HEIHWA01

"My current organization offers me the best infrastructure, logistics and mentorship. I enjoy working with my colleagues and students. Although working with many power heads is often challenging, I feel it has taught me new skills"

Name: **Organization:**
Prof. (Dr.) Nigam Dave   **Academics**

☺Happy Experience☺Work Ambience☺HEIHWA02

"whenever I feel frustrated and if I start to feel that my life is going monotonous, I spend my time with my students who with their frankness and jolliness change my mood, which allows me to focus on my work as my mind gets fresh and I can start my work afresh. Hence this environment allows me to de-stress and achieve perfect outcome of my work"

Name: **Organization:**
Surabhi Poduval **Academics**

☺Happy Experience☺Work Ambience☺HEIHWA03

"I like the work environment over here like flexible timing, providing proper training which makes me happy to work. As I am married and also a mother of a 5 year old kid, I have to give attention to my family and kid when they want. So, accordingly I can adjust my time here. Also once I want to learn English through a course, which my organization allowed me by approving half day contribution to the course which makes me happy and satisfied"

Name: **Organization:**
Hetal J tripathi **HR Consultancy Firm**

☺Happy Experience☺Work Ambience☺HEIHWA04

"All staff person are very familiar over here. All member always supports each other in any difficult. If anyone becomes absent then all other will help in his/her work. Hitesh uncle always considers us as small kids and teaches so many things. Ravi bhai and Dipak always helps staff for extra work. And Lucky sir always gives positive feeling for work. I have never seen a boss like Lucky sir as he never had a negative aspect in life"

Name: **Organization:**
Hiren Sakarval **Service Industry**

☺Happy Experience☺Work Ambience☺HEIHWA05

"The work environment is very satisfactory. Company provides flexible hours; we get radio facility entire day, satisfactory sitting arrangement, clear work space and area. The people travelling from distant area get good scope of working along with handling household responsibility"

Name: **Organization:**
Stuti   **HR Consultancy Firm**

We have seen the dimension Individual happiness. Let us try to understand the next dimension Individual Unhappiness.

Dimension 2: Individual Unhappiness

Work environment

Challenges faced by you at your work place are indicated here. It includes your skills, nature, computer illiteracy, and performance. Infrastructure, system and processes of place, colleagues, rewards and work culture also plays a major role.

Work Environment sub factors are Facilities, System & Process, Appreciation, Performance, and Impatient Nature & Computer Literacy.

Self-Adequacy

It indicates your ability to perform at work. It includes your nature being perfectionist/short-tempered overaggressive. It also includes your inadequate knowledge or skills of work.

Self-Adequacy's sub factors are Skills, Over aggressive nature, Short tempered, Nature, Inadequate job knowledge & Perfectionist.

Work demand

This signifies demanding nature of your job. Workload, deadline pressures, work timings and stress due to work are included here.

Work demand's sub factors are Work Pressure, Target / Deadline pressure, Stress, work timings

Work culture

It explains your internal working environment that can motivate/demotivate you to perform better. It includes factors like behavior of boss, biasness, colleagues, monotonous work, and politics around, your job profile and work environment.

Work Culture sub factors are politics, Monotonous job, Boss, Work Environment, and Biasness & Colleagues.

Job Satisfaction

Different facets of job like salary, work life balance, job profile and time for own self determines job satisfaction.

Job Satisfaction sub factors are Salary, Time for self & Job Profile

After getting through the Individual Happiness & Unhappiness understanding we now look at the next dimension of Happiness which is Family / Social Happiness.

Dimension 3: Family/Social happiness

Home and social environment

It indicates family and social support system that helps you to carry out your job effectively. It includes factors like appreciation from helpful and loving family, spouse and children support, encouragement, cooperation of family and friends, freedom for job and positive home environment.

Home / Social Environment sub factors are Freedom for job, encouraging family, loving family, Helpful Family, Spouse support, Co – operative family, Positive approach, Children support, Support for job, Friends.

Some of the real time experiences shared by respondents, which highlight the examples of this cluster, are as follows:

☺Happy Experience ☺Home/Social Environment ☺HESHSE01

"Because of my current job I am well recognized within my relatives as well as neighbors, which was not there in past as they looked at me as only a 12th pass but now my status is high"

Name: **Organization:**
Hasanabbas N Momin   **Retail Supermarket**

☺Happy Experience ☺Home/Social Environment ☺HESHSE02

"From my family side I have no responsibility so I am not over- burdened in my job. Even though I am married than also I am relaxed from my family side. I live in a joint family so everyone helps each other if any problem occurs and hence I am able to survive in my job"

Name: **Organization:**
Patel Nilam Maulik **Academics**

☺Happy Experience ☺Home/Social Environment ☺HESHSE03

"Being from a family that not only supports but also encourages career of a married woman and a mother of a toddler, it is really a matter of pride. No time constraints, no restrictions when it comes to requirement of a job make me a happy individual overall"

Name: **Organization:**
Ranna Vaishnav **Academics**

☺Happy Experience ☺Home/Social Environment ☺HESHSE04

"Staying almost 25kms away from my work place, my 9 hours job turns into 12 hours because of travelling. My family accepts it and supports me. At the end of the day, I get tired and stressed, but on reaching home I don't have any additional responsibilities to fulfill. So that I can fulfill my professional duties properly"

Name: **Organization:**
Kavya Basantani **Academics**

☺Happy Experience ☺Home/Social Environment ☺HESHSE05

"We are living in a joint family where my grandfather is a doctor; my father in law is a government law employee whereas my mother in law is a housewife. So, they want me to be a workingwoman because earlier my mother in law got an opportunity to do a job but she was not having support from her family, so they know the importance of a job. They motivate me and also take care of my child & that makes me very happy"

Name: **Organization:**
Hetal J Tripathi   **HR Consultancy Firm**

☺Happy Experience ☺Home/Social Environment ☺HESHSE06

"Once I was on tour of Lucknow & there I had to work late night. I was so frustrated, due to the problem I was not about to troubleshoot. At that time, I received a call from my mother, she empathize me and I felt some relief. After that, I troubleshoot that problem very easily"

Name: **Organization:**
Amit Shukla   **Manufacturing Sector**

☺Happy Experience ☺Home/Social Environment ☺HESHSE07

"In my company whenever I need some immediate leave for exams or some other cause, my company always grants it and just because of that reason my family supports me whenever I have to stay in office for long time. So this combination also makes me happy"

Name: **Organization:**
Hiren Sakarval   **Service Sector**

Family support

It shows motivation and encouragement received from immediate family members towards your job. It includes support, understanding and encouragement from family.

Family Support Sub factors are Encouraging Family, understanding family, Motivating family support.

Some of the real time experiences shared by respondents, which highlight the examples of this cluster, are as follows:

☺Happy Experience☺Family Support☺HESHFS01

"I am staying out of home/family and it is very difficult to maintain the expectations of family but still I am getting best support from my parents as when should I go home and meet them or they come to meet me if I am busy with my work. I am able to balance my family and work life thanks to my family"

Name: **Organization:**
Vibhuti Kiri   **Service Sector**

☺Happy Experience☺Family Support☺HESHFS02

"My work place is in Baroda which is a 2 hour drive in bus from my home. Hence I preferred to stay as a paying guest at Baroda. My family supported me throughout the dilemma whether I should stay home doing up-down or stay as a PG (Paying Guest). Their support had eased my decision"

Name: Pinky   **Organization:**
(name changed)   **Academics**

☺Happy Experience☺Family Support☺HESHFS03

"I have a small family which understands the complexity and challenges of my work and support me to focus totally on my work. They don't share small problems they face so that I can concentrate on my work. To succeed one has to focus more either on work or on family. I feel lucky that I can focus on work as my family encourages & supports me to do that."

Name: **Organization:**
Prof. (Dr.) Nigam Dave   **Academics**

☺Happy Experience☺Family Support☺HESHFS04

"Since my profession is very common these days and require constant new thinking/mindset so that my students don't get bored I require a constant guidance from my family who were my first teacher. They guide me to make me understand various aspects of the child's psychology, which helps me to get attached with my students. Since my sister is also a professor of a well-known institute, she guides me well for this job"

Name: **Organization:**
Surabhi Poduval   **Academics**

☺Happy Experience☺Family Support☺HESHFS05

"It is always pleasing and encouraging when family members support me in terms of even understanding my unavailability at an important gathering. I was unable to attend my real brother's engagement but still I was in spirits and my family stood by me then."

Name: **Organization:**
Tapann K Joshi   **Academics**

☺Happy Experience☺Family Support☺HESHFS06

"I was initially working in my family business and I was earning better than what I am earning right now which is three times less but my family supported to work me here i.e. which is of my field and first step to my goal i.e. to become a practicing CS"

Name: **Organization:**
Zalak Jainish Shah **Finance Sector**

☺Happy Experience☺Family Support☺HESHFS07

"I have a huge family support for example my daughter who is a B.Com graduate is able to keep me updated with her new knowledge about recent studies and also it helps me a lot because it creates a good image of mine in my job"

Name: **Organization:**
R H Vyas **Government Office**

☺Happy Experience☺Family Support☺HESHFS08

"My mother as well as my mother in law both are very supportive. I can share my problems with my father who gives me suggestions. My family supports me a lot if I have to come late at night. Even I share my problems with my husband; he listens and guides me for my problem"

Name: **Organization:**
Rajal Patel **Service Sector**

Openness

Openness suggests extent to which you can share your work life with your family members. It not only includes family support but also sharing of problems and receiving guidance. Family culture plays a major role here.

Openness sub factors are support in job, Sharing problems & guidance, Family culture.

Some of the real time experiences shared by respondents, which highlight the examples of this cluster, are as follows:

☺Happy Experience☺Openness☺HESHO01

"Need to work from home sometimes, receiving/making work related calls, preparing for classes @ home has made the environment such that every family member can relate and understand what is going on at work."

Name: **Organization:**
Ranna Vaishnav   **Academics**

☺Happy Experience☺Openness☺HESHO02

"One day in my current organization, one of my colleagues took my personal number without informing me and started irritating by calling me. I really don't like this kind of behavior, so I discussed this with my family and everyone supported me and motivated me to be confident and not get affected by it."

Name: **Organization:**
Patel Nilam Maulik   **Academics**

☺Happy Experience☺Openness☺HESHO03

"Once in my job, my colleagues made a big scene out of my frankness with my students which made me blue. I was very upset with the thought that still people are not open to the new way of teaching. I shared it with my family who understood the situation very well and made me think that every new way is always criticized at first, which firmed my decision that I will continue with my work and my new technique and further more I started to take different perceptions for problems in my life"

Name: **Organization:**
Surabhi Poduval   **Academics**

☺Happy Experience☺Openness☺HESHO04

"I used to share my job profile, stress and environment with my family. Once I started with this job, it was really tough to cope up with the target, at that time my mother in law advised me to generate passion for the job because anything you learn from this job will give you stability and will give you more focus which will improve you day by day. She also told me not to take any stress because every day would not be same which motivated me to perform well and do well in my job"

Name: **Organization:**
Hetal J Tripathi   **HR Consultancy Firm**

☺Happy Experience☺Openness☺HESHO05

"I share all my happening at office with my mother. When recently one of my colleague left job and it was her birthday 2 to 3 days prior she left organization, we bought flowers, pastry, decorated the board of office, her PC, gave her gift and made her feel special as she was youngest in experience as well as age amongst all the team members, I shared entire day happening with my mom which made me feel happy as well nostalgic"

Name: **Organization:**
Stuti   **HR Consultancy Firm**

Social Support

It explains family support received to maintain social commitments/status as well as work demands. It includes cooperation of family by adjusting timings, sharing responsibilities and supporting emotionally.

Social support sub factors are sharing responsibility, Social Status, Emotional support & Adjustment of timing.

Some of the real time experiences shared by respondents, which highlight the examples of this cluster, are as follows:

☺Happy Experience☺Social Support☺HESHSS01

"There are many functions going on in the society like marriages in the family and *pooja* at home. Sometimes I am not able to go to home as I have a tight schedule or month end or there are Sundays and Sundays are very busy for me; but I always got support from my family and they are encouraging me to focus on what I should do"

Name: **Organization:**
Vibhuti Kiri   **Service sector**

☺Happy Experience☺Social Support☺HESHSS02

"At the time of March ending or in the season of advance tax/audit, I have to sit in office for late nights say 2 or 3:00

AM maybe for 10-12 days. That means my office hours increased to 15 hours from 7 hours. For working so late with full efficiency for which I needed support of my family as well as socially. My family supported me and allowed me for late nights. Ultimately what I was doing was only for building my career and that's what family and society wants."

Name: Krushit
Kaushikbhai Shah

Organization:
Finance sector

☺Happy Experience☺Social Support☺HESHSS03

"One day a coincidence happened that I have to reach office by 10:30 and also have to go to my son's office to pick him up at his school by 11:30. It created a very crucial situation for me as both the situation were colliding so I called my sister in law to pick my son and later I can pick him up and take him home. Sister in law also plays an important role in my job"

Name: Shraddha
(name changed)

Organization:
HR Consultancy Firm

☺Happy Experience☺Social Support☺HESHSS04

"My family always motivates me to work better, because sometime I feel lazy and don't want to go to work or leave job for silly reason. That time my family helps me a lot. My friends work with me and provide me co-operation and also motivate me to work hard, thus I am able to survive any difficult situation"

Name:
Ruchir Mehta

Organization:
IT Firm

Networking

It indicates connection with people socially, connection with colleagues and a good network of people with you.

Networking sub factors are colleagues & Network.

Some of the real time experiences shared by respondents, which highlight the examples of this cluster, are as follows:

☺Happy Experience☺Networking☺HESHN01

"After many years I am able to learn excel and tally, so when any of my friends call me to know about tally or excel it really makes me very happy and makes me feel as if I am able to become valuable for some one's knowledge addition."

Name: Imran   Organization:
Siddikhbhai Sindhi   Retail Supermarket

☺Happy Experience☺Networking☺HESHN02

"Just because of this company I am able to meet important persons like Lucky sir, even I extent my network in Reliance telecommunication department also like Rajnish Malhotra who is Gujarat head person for retention department in Reliance, even so many corporate friends like Ricky mam, Rohan, Dharti etc. expanded my valuable network."

Name: Organization:
Hiren Sakarval   Service Sector

☺Happy Experience☺Networking☺HESHN03

"We, the staffs, are all socially active. We share our personal things with each other and encourage each other in pursuing our passion, listen out each other. This makes us more connected. Even company organizes one day tour for employees so that we get comfortable and enjoy the work"

Name: Kavya Basantani   **Organization: Academics**

☺Happy Experience☺Networking☺HESHN04

"Things that I like most is interacting with various people. I am an extrovert and nature of my work allows me social interaction with all stakeholders which may not be possible otherwise. I network with my management, colleagues, students, parents, government, media and non-technical staff. This provides me ample opportunity to learn new skills everyday"

Name: **Organization:**
Prof. (Dr.) Nigam Dave   **Academics**

☺Happy Experience☺Networking☺HESHN05

"At some time after working with people for long period of time say 4-5 months, you get connected professionally as well as emotional with that person. My office environment is not so liberal but at least articles/employees at the same stage talk and discuss with each other that helps each other to solve their professional as well as social problems. It is because we spent most of our time in office and so we know them personally and we can help them."

Name: Krushit   **Organization:**
Kaushikbhai Shah   **Finance Sector**

☺Happy Experience☺Networking☺HESHN06

"To be able to connect to as many people as possible has always been something which I have longed for. Today because of my work, I am a known name in quite a few colleges and in the academic industry across Ahmedabad as well as nearby areas"

Name: **Organization:**
Tapann K Joshi   **Academics**

☺Happy Experience☺Networking☺HESHN07

"I like to be a happy go lucky person and I do interact with my colleague when we have lunch together. I share about work and get many opportunities to explore also. We share birthday parties, events which makes me interact more with people which I enjoy a lot"

Name: Meera   **Organization:**
(name changed)   **HR Consultancy Firm**

☺Happy Experience☺Networking☺HESHN08

"Recently, one of my team members shared her personal problems she faced after her marriage which was a new thing for her. I guided her and shared my similar problems where I underwent similar financial/family or social problems. It helped us both."

Name: **Organization:**
Stuti   **HR Consultancy Firm**

☺Happy Experience☺Networking☺HESHN09

"I connect with all age groups. Networking in our office is very easy as we have the platform to interact with each other in ways of a common agenda like training, social gathering, employee engagements where interactions are freely exchanged. This helps us build ourselves"

Name: **Organization:**
Sarita Bhat   **HR Consultancy Firm**

☺**Happy Experience**☺**Networking**☺**HESHN10**

"I have a huge network with different domains. My big group include people with same technology & different technology domains and I get latest information and faster learning from my network."

Name: **Organization:**

Dhruvit Rajpura   **IT firm**

Dimension 4: Family/Social unhappiness

Home and Social environment

It indicates family and social challenges that impact your job. Health, nature and demands of family members, disturbance at work, problems due to relatives and family commitments, impact your work life.

Home & Social Environment sub factors are Family Problem, Nature of family members, Health of Family, Reaching office time, Responsibilities of Family, Disturbance at work time, Family commitment at work, Relatives & Demanding Family.

Family support

It explains challenges faced by your family that affects your job. It includes nature of family members, financial insecurity, out stationed family, non-understanding family members and interpersonal relations with family members.

Family support sub factors are Lack of support, Financial security, Interpersonal relations in family, Mobiles, Family out stationed & Not understanding

Self-Helplessness

It shows your personal feeling of being inadequate to meet social and family commitments. It includes time for your children, friend, family and self. It also indicates your work load, stress and work life balance.

Self-Helplessness sub factors are Time for self, Time for children, Time for friends, Time for social / Family life & Stress.

Dimension 5: Organizational happiness

Work environment

It shows extent to which internal work environment and work culture boosts your performance. It includes system and processes, growth opportunities, support from seniors, upgraded technologies, management, positive environment and ambience.

Work Environment sub factors are Professional, Support, Ambience, Work culture, Technologically upgraded, Positive, Seniors & System and process.

Some of the real time experiences shared by respondents, which highlight the examples of this cluster, are as follows:

☺Happy Experience ☺Work Environment ☺HEOHWE01

"Once I was confused how to update our software for further stage but my business colleague and my immediate senior helped me and explained once again. Like-wise in many situations where I got stuck they help me to come out of that."

Name: Tamanna **Organization:**
(name changed) **HR Consultancy firm**

☺Happy Experience ☺Work Environment ☺HEOHWE02

"My internal team members helped me a lot when I was new to this company. In one position I didn't get any resumes or any keywords to find CVs, at that time my team members helped me for that and finally I got CVs and filled the position."

Name: **Organization:**
Pooja K Panchal **HR Consultancy firm**

☺Happy Experience☺Work Environment☺HEOHWE03

"Internal work plays an important role as it tends to interact with like and unlike minded people. If the work environment gives us freedom to work, without much stress, it automatically instills a sense of responsibility in me to complete my task as per the given target. Even the interest to complete the work, due to the encouragement at work, assist in building happiness and in turn performing at work"

Name: **Organization:**
Sarita Bhat **HR Consultancy firm**

Organizational Support

It indicates the extent to which your work environment and support increase your performance. It includes friendly environment, support from boss and colleagues, freedom of work and safe and healthy environment.

Organizational support sub factors are Friendly, Colleagues, Freedom / Autonomy, Safe & healthy & Boss.

Some of the real time experiences shared by respondents, which highlight the examples of this cluster, are as follows:

☺Happy Experience ☺Organizational Support ☺HEOHOS01

"If I lack in motivation or I am not able to give what I am expected to then I am always getting best support from my boss and he is just a call away. I thank to my boss for motivating me by calling on intervals or arranging training related to that or arranging shadowing with the seniors"

Name: **Organization:**
Vibhuti Kiri   **Service Sector**

☺Happy Experience ☺Organizational Support ☺HEOHOS02

"I am from the IT sector. My work is to promote the brand in social media so when I am confused in some situation then the organization gives me full support and helps to provide solution. They give certain ideas. They provide me certain data regarding the problem and give me motivation whenever I am going wrong in certain places"

Name: **Organization:**
Maysamali Momin   **Retail Supermarket**

☺Happy Experience ☺Organizational Support ☺HEOHOS03

"Just two months old in organization, my boss called me for a meeting. First he appreciated me for my sincerity towards work and then he guided me on how to improve myself. Not only did he guide me how I should continue with my passion towards art but also how I should make a goal for life. I am very grateful to get such a leader as my boss"

Name: Kavya Basantani   Organization: Academics

☺Happy Experience☺Organizational Support☺HEOHOS04

"This organization gives freedom to work and with responsibilities it gives me self-satisfaction to work more. At workplace apart from giving mental support it also gives facility of listening to music which improves productivity on work also"

Name: Meera   Organization:
(name changed)   HR Consultancy Firm

☺Happy Experience ☺Organizational Support ☺HEOHOS05

"Due to some personal reason I have to leave my job from technical domain for six months. After six months, when I rejoined there were no vacancy in the technical domain. So my company transferred me to IT domain, which gave me one more opportunity to work again in this organization. And also I was given training and understanding for this job profile."

Name: Organization:
Hetal J tripathi   HR Consultancy Firm

☺Happy Experience ☺Organizational Support ☺HEOHOS06

"Once I was stuck at site late night for our client. At that time I had no idea what to do what not to. So, I called my regional head about this matter. Although it was almost 3 o clock at night, he gave me the solution"

Name: **Organization:**
Amit Shukla   **Manufacturing Sector**

Self-Growth

It explains the extent to which your company has contributed to your personal and professional development. It includes training and development, learning and growth opportunities and exposure provided by your company. It includes your social status as well.

Self-Growth sub factors are Training & development, Social Status, Learning opportunities & expose & brand name.

Some of the real time experiences shared by respondents, which highlight the examples of this cluster, are as follows:

☺Happy Experience☺Self Growth☺HEOHSG01

"Starting as a fresher, then graduating to a faculty and then as a mentor on faculty side of my role and handling schedules of a complex system that is spread in different locations is something I had never expected of my own self a few years back"

Name: **Organization:**
Ranna Vaishnav   **Academics**

☺**Happy Experience☺Self Growth☺HEOHSG02**

"When I joined this company, my drafting skills were not so good but with the help of my colleagues who corrected my mistakes, I am now able to do drafting every well. I am able to convince our candidate on salary part i.e. negotiating with them for right figure. I have learnt a lot about corporate world from this organization"

Name: Shruti   **Organization:**
(name changed)   **HR Consultancy Firm**

☺**Happy Experience☺Self Growth☺HEOHSG03**

"I believe I am a product of the organization that I have worked for. They have enriched my understanding of life and its intricacies. I believe what you learn by incidents and events have a lasting effect on others and are important as it brings a sense of maturity and satisfaction from your very own self."

Name: Kashish   **Organization:**
(name changed)   **Academics**

☺**Happy Experience☺Self Growth☺HEOHSG04**

"Workplace which allows me to work with creativity, confidence and clarity, results in self-growth. I am a privileged person as my former government job provided me clarity and my current job allows working with creativity and confidence. Organizational goals at my current workplace keep on setting new milestones which keep me on my toes and help me grow every year."

Name: **Organization:**
Prof. (Dr.) Nigam Dave   **Academics**

☺Happy Experience☺Self Growth☺HEOHSG05

"In this world every person is greedy which I believe and it pretty well worked for me. In the office we deal with every type of problems which helps me a lot in my CA final examination. In the exam I need theoretical as well as practical knowledge. Theoretical gain is from reading but the practical knowledge is attained from my article-ship. Books just give us instructions but practical approach leads us to think out of the box."

Name: Krushit Kaushikbhai Shah

Organization: Finance Sector

☺Happy Experience☺Self Growth☺HEOHSG06

"My Company motivated us to go through a lot of training which led me to do PGDSHRM and understand and increase my opportunity further in this field and it is possible only because of my organization's support. I had done my project from my organization and they also shared with me their company manual. This course changed my perspective and value added to my profile also."

Name: Hetal J Tripathi

Organization: HR Consultancy Firm

☺Happy Experience☺Self Growth☺HEOHSG07

"My company is arranging various types of training and events so I get a lot of knowledge in various areas. My company has given me a chance to change my field for better growth"

Name: Pooja K Panchal

Organization: HR Consultancy Firm

☺**Happy Experience**☺**Self Growth**☺**HEOHSG08**

"My career is developing and has reached at quite a high level as my company is growing which led me to contact lot of people, who guided me and with their co-operation I am able to grow professionally."

Name: **Organization:**
Rajal Patel   **Manufacturing Firm**

☺**Happy Experience**☺**Self Growth**☺**HEOHSG09**

"I joined as a fresher into HR but each day has given me new knowledge and new milestone. They have given me knowledge about all prospects of recruitment. I gained good knowledge of all kind of profiles, industry, etc. Now I am more knowledgeable about HR policies."

Name: **Organization:**
Stuti   **HR Consultancy Firm**

Organizational Policies

It indicates the extent to which you feel your company's HR Policies are favorable to you. It includes work culture, growth opportunities, flexible work timings and politics on job.

Organizational Policies sub factors are Flexible timings, Politics, HR, and Growth Opportunities.

Some of the real time experiences shared by respondents, which highlight the examples of this cluster, are as follows:

☺**Happy Experience** ☺**Organizational Policies** ☺**HEOHOP01**

"Being married and also a mother, flexible timing plays an important role in my life which I got from my company's

HR policy. I just have to complete 8.5 hours of time slot and then can go home. Leave policy is also superb as I can have hassle free leaves."

Name: Shraddha   **Organization:**
(name changed)   **HR Consultancy Firm**

☺Happy Experience ☺Organizational Policies ☺HEOHOP02

"If policies of an organization support its employee, it automatically increases the ability and contribution of an employee to his work and organization. If employee has assurance about the policies of company that help him to secure and boost up his career, he is able to work properly and in best possible manner."

Name: Ricky   **Organization:**
(name changed)   **IT Firm**

☺Happy Experience ☺Organizational Policies ☺HEOHOP03

"I found that my organization has some policies where I can find myself as employee & not just like a worker For example: (1) We have insurance policies which helps to secure myself. (2) The other policies are same as others like leave, increment and terminate; and the best thing they do is some events to explore our inner talents."

Name: Vaibhav   **Organization:**
Jayantibhai Solanki   **IT Firm**

Employee engagement

It indicates the focus your company's maintenance to keep employees motivated and aligned. It includes extra activities, motivation, encouragement, growth opportunities and responsibilities.

Employee Engagement sub factors are Extracurricular activities, Responsibility, Exposure, Motivation & Appreciation / Reward.

Some of the real time experiences shared by respondents, which highlight the examples of this cluster, are as follows:

☺Happy Experience ☺Employee Engagement ☺HEOHEE01

"Our company organizes tour/ meeting/ outings to keep employee motivated. Directors take part in it. Takes suggestions from all the employees and discuss all the decisions. This makes us an integral part of company, which keeps us motivated."

Name: Kavya Basantani   Organization: Academics

☺Happy Experience ☺Employee Engagement ☺HEOHEE02

"I am working in a company where employees are too many and many of them are not able to meet each other, so for meeting the employees they always arrange a meeting/ training/ business reviews where all the employees can meet each other and share their experiences and learn something from each other."

Name: Organization:
Vibhuti Kiri   Service Sector

☺Happy Experience ☺Employee Engagement ☺HEOHEE03

"For any organization, employees are the true assets of the organization. Employees are the persons who do the work on time and in perfect manner. Once, we were not able to complete the work on time and so we decided to put that work on side. But at the time our sir came into picture, discussed with us the problem and helped us in solving the problem and then we finally completed the work. At that time our motivation was that our sir is working with us."

Name: Krushit   **Organization:**
Kaushikbhai Shah   **Finance Sector**

☺Happy Experience ☺Employee Engagement ☺HEOHEE04

"Many of my colleagues are much older to me and they gained more experience than I had, which allowed to gain more guidance, more solutions for different problems as well as to cope up with different organizational politics. My colleagues also welcomed me with warm heart which made me feel at home."

Name: **Organization:**
Surabhi Poduval   **Academics**

☺Happy Experience ☺Employee Engagement ☺HEOHEE05

"Every day was a challenge for me at work place as it was altogether new type of work. But due to support and motivation from my sir I am able to reach to this level where I can handle the work alone. Just because of support and

motivation from Anjali madam and Shaunak sir, made me capable of doing work at a faster pace."
Name: Zalak Jainish Shah   Organization: Finance Sector

☺Happy Experience ☺Employee Engagement ☺HEOHEE06

"Our company does events I think that might help me to remember that I am working with this organization, they give rewards and take photographs of every employee and also put them on our website. so I too got recognition once & that really makes me happy as I can now show my family where I am working and I am valued."
Name: VaibhavJayantibhai   Organization:
Solanki   IT Firm

Job Role

It signifies the extent to which your job duties and remuneration motivates you at work.

Job Role sub factors are Job Profile & Salary.

Some of the real time experiences shared by respondents, which highlight the examples of this cluster, are as follows:

☺Happy Experience☺Job Role☺HEOHJR01

"I am working in the retention department of reliance telecommunication and in this job we always meet the person who are already negative for Reliance. So to convince them for continuing Reliance service is just like changing human mindset which is pretty tough, but I like it most because it improves my convincing power."
Name: Hiren Sakarval   Organization: Service Sector

☺Happy Experience☺Job Role☺HEOHJR02

"When you are a founder of an organization and not just an employee, job becomes much more than duty. My current role has given me immense happiness and satisfaction as from the roots I could see my organization flourish. God has been gracious on me as in my previous job I was a second only employee whereas in my current organization I started it. Passing through the project phase and seeing through teething problems has given me enough challenges and equally enough happiness"

Name: **Organization:**
Prof. (Dr.) Nigam Dave   **Academics**

☺Happy Experience☺Job Role☺HEOHJR03

"Yes, the duties and remuneration are 2 best factors. After coming to office I perform my job role and it is the only thing, which motivates me. The remuneration is need of every one in job. When I get salary and meet my domestic needs it reduces all pressures of job."

Name: **Organization:**
Stuti   **HR Consultancy Firm**

☺Happy Experience☺Job Role☺HEOHJR04

"Duties do give me sense of responsibility and seniority. At this age I am leading a whole discussion of the company which really pleases me. Remuneration is good though, but more is always welcome."

Name: **Organization:**
Gaurav Vesasi   **Manufacturing Firm**

Work Life Balance

It indicates the extent to which your company supports you to maintain your work life balance. It includes factors like week offs and leaves, job security and less pressure.

Work Life Balance sub factors are Week offs and leaves, Job Security and less pressure.

Some of the real time experiences shared by respondents, which highlight the examples of this cluster, are as follows:

☺Happy Experience ☺Work-Life Balance ☺HEOHWB01

"Whenever I have personal issues and with honesty if I go about it and share it with my management then we are able to prioritize and concentrate on our issues. This in turn motivates us to perform our best at work. Understanding and empathizing with situation by our management / organization is very important."

Name: **Organization:**
Sarita Bhat   **HR Consultancy Firm**

☺Happy Experience ☺Work-Life Balance ☺HEOHWB02

"I can commute at evening by 4:00 pm and even when I want to see my family I take half day and visit my family and friends whenever I want. Hence I am able to provide time for my family as well as for my work as there are no restrictions or limitations."

Name: Pinky   **Organization:**
(name changed)   **Academics**

☺Happy Experience ☺Work-Life Balance ☺HEOHWB03

"At any moment of time if I have to attend my son's school twice or thrice, then I take TL from my office. Therefore I am able to handle my son's happiness and I am also able to attend office after his school which is very helpful for me."

Name: Shraddha   **Organization:**
(name changed)   **HR Consultancy Firm**

Dimension 6: Organizational unhappiness

Work Environment

It indicates the challenges at your work place that impact your job performance. It includes distance from home, salary cuts, domination, colleagues, support, unhealthy competition, freedom etc.

Work Environment sub factors are Colleagues, Support, Dominating, Salary cuts, Salary, Distance from home, Freedom / Autonomy, Unhealthy competition, Work Environment & Colleagues.

Employee Orientation.

It indicates lack of concern for employee in organization's approach to work.

In includes performance parameters, work allocation, indecisiveness, work culture, system and process, facilities, management, interdepartmental co-ordination and HR.

Employee Orientation sub factors are Performance parameters, HR, Interdepartmental co-ordination, Indecisiveness m Work culture, System & Process, Facilities & Management.

Job Role and Demands

It indicates the impact of nature of job demands on job effectiveness. It includes work load, work timings, job profile clarity, performance, politics, communication gap, monotonous job and system and process.

Job Role & Demands sub factors are Work load, Work timings, Monotonous Job, Job Profile Clarity, Performance, Politics, system & Process & Communication Gap.

Organizational Support.

It indicates organizational constraints that hinder employee performance. It includes appreciation/reward, growth opportunities and transparency in work culture.

Organizational Support sub factors are Appreciation / Reward, Growth opportunities & Transparency.

What's Next?

In case you have paid attention to examples cited and the explanation of the 3D-model of happiness, you would have come across many factors that you might have correlated yourself with. It is something that each one of encounters every day.

In fact the 3D model of happiness is arrived at through research and survey of over 800 employees and thus it reflects the actual situation and experiences as well as factors that determine happiness and unhappiness at work.

Thus the next obvious question would be how to determine these factors? You can determine these factors using the happiness inventory given in the next section.

3

Happiness Inventory

We have given here abridged inventory for you to partially identify your happiness factors. For a detailed understanding and attempting the complete 164-factor inventory, you will need to attempt it online on www.choosehappiness.in or get in touch with Dr. Yogesh Pahuja on Yogesh.pahuja@gmail.com

The abridged inventory includes the following dimensions and clusters. About 30 sub factors are taken into consideration:

Dimension	Cluster	No of Sub factors
Individual Happiness	Affiliation	*07*
Individual Unhappiness	Self-adequacy	06
Social/ Family Happiness	Openness	03
Social/ Family Unhappiness	Family Support	06
Organizational Happiness	Employee Engagement	05
Organizational Unhappiness	Organizational Support	03

In this section, the Happiness Inventory consists of 3 parts:

i) **DIY – H.i. (a):** Do it yourself – happiness inventory (abridged). This includes a questionnaire where you can tick mark your choice of response as per the instructions.

ii) **Scoring Sheet:** This will help you mark your obtained score against Total Score.

iii) **Interpretation Norms and Abridged Report:** Here we have given report template where you can fill it in as per the instructions and find out how you fare as per the gender and age wise norms given.

i) DIY – H.i. (a) – Do it yourself Happiness Inventory (abridged)

Instructions:

1. Do not leave any question blank.
2. Read each statement and tick mark your answer choice against each statement
3. Use scale below to mark your choice.

Tick mark:

0	If you never or rarely feel this way
1	If you occasionally feel this way
2	If you sometimes feel this way
3	If you frequently feel this way
4	If you very frequently or always feel this way

Please Note: This is an abridged inventory, for full version please visit: www.choosehappiness.in

Name:	
Age:	Gender: M/ F
Organization Name:	
Sector:	Total Experience (Years):

Section IH (Individual Happiness)

Affiliation						
Sr. No.		0	1	2	3	4
1	I like the systems and processes of my organization.					
2	I have a clear vision of my organization.					
3	My boss and seniors are willing to help.					
4	My company's name is among best brands.					
5	I trust my team and my organization.					
6	The faith and support of the management helps me at work.					
7	The work timings are most appropriate for me.					
Total Score				Max Score		28

Section IUH (Individual Unhappiness)

Self-Adequacy						
Sr. No.		0	1	2	3	4
8	Due to lack of certain skills my effectiveness is less at work.					
9	My over aggressive nature affects my performance.					
10	I am short tempered due to which I face problems at work.					
11	Certain traits of my personality affect my performance and professional relations.					
12	My lack of job knowledge affects my performance.					
13	My urge for perfection and improvement disturbs my performance.					
Total Score				Max Score		24

Section SH (Social/Family Happiness)

Openness		0	1	2	3	4
Sr. No.						
14	My family takes interest in my daily happenings at office.					
15	I share my office problems with my family & they try to solve it & guide me.					
16	My family background helps me to share job related issues with them.					
Total Score				Max Score		12

Section SUH (Social/Family Unhappiness)

Family Support						
Sr. No.		0	1	2	3	4
17	I face lack of support from my family.					
18	My family is financially insecure.					
19	My family members do not get along well with each other.					
20	I wish my mobile was banned at office.					
21	Being away from family affects my performance at work					
22	My family members do not understand my job requirements and me.					
Total Score				Max Score		24

Section OH (Organizational Happiness)

Employee Engagement		0	1	2	3	4
Sr. No.		0	1	2	3	4
23	There are extracurricular activities & celebrations at my work place.					
24	My organization provides opportunities to take higher responsibilities.					
25	My organization provides exposure in different functional areas.					
26	There is motivation to excel & improve at my organization.					
27	Good performance & efforts are appreciated and rewarded in my organization.					
Total Score				Max Score		20

Section OUH (Organizational Unhappiness)

Organizational Support						
Sr. No.		0	1	2	3	4
28	There is lack of appreciation and rewards on good performance in my company.					
29	Growth opportunities for employees provided by my organization are limited.					
30	There is lack of transparency at my work place.					
	Total Score			Max Score		12

ii) Scoring Sheet

Instructions:

1. Once you are done attempting the questionnaire, total the scores cluster wise and fill it the column 'Total Score' below.
2. Enter the total score for each cluster in the Scoring Sheet below.

Dimension	Cluster	Total Score	Max Score
IH	Affiliation		28
IUH	Self-Adequacy		24
SH	Openness		12
SUH	Family Support		24
OH	Employee Engagement		20
OUH	Organizational Support		12

iii) Interpretation- Norms and Abridged Report

Instructions:

- Write your cluster score into header row.
- Shade your score in the sub factor table based on your tick mark made in the questionnaire. Keep the same order while marking the score. For example affiliation's questionnaire's first statement's you have marked score as 3, than reflect the same by shading the No1 sub factor (Systems & Processes).

How to read:

- This is a cluster wise report.
- The header row indicates your obtained score which indicates your status such as Low/ Average/ High.
- The definition of the cluster is explained.
- Below the definition a norms table indicates the ideal score based on gender and age bracket. You can compare your happiness score here.
- The Next table gives the sub factors and your score against each.

Note: This abridged report only gives you the score, definition of cluster, the norms and the sub factor score. It helps you to identify the sub factor and the table tells you if your score was high or low or average across a sample of 500-tested population. This report should NOT be used to draw any inferences or make any critical decisions.

IH Cluster- Affiliation: (Extent to which I feel connected to/ with my work place.)

Your Score: ____/28   (Low: 0-7, Average: 8-21,
(fill it from scoring sheet)   High: 22-28)

Affiliation:

Affiliation indicates the extent to which you feel connection/ association with your organization in which you work. Affiliation includes factors like, your work culture including the system & its progress, the support you get from your boss & seniors, the brand name of your organization, your work timings, trust on team and organization and vision clarity.

Norms:

Individual - Gender and Age wise Norms (N=500, m=381 & f=119)						
Range	Low		Average		High	
Gender	Male	Female	Male	Female	Male	Female
Norms	16	17	17-20	18-21	21	22
Range	Low		Average		High	
Age	Greater than 35 years	Less than 35 years	Greater than 35 years	Less than 35 years	Greater than 35 years	Less than 35 years
Norms	17	15	18-22	16-20	23	21

Sub factor:

Statement No	Sub Factor	Your Score (Shade the boxes)				
		0	**1**	**2**	**3**	**4**
Example: (if your score is 3)		▨	▨	▨	▨	
1	System & Process					
2	Vision Clarity					
3	Boss & Seniors					
4	Brand Name					
5	Trust on Team & Organization					
6	Management Support					
7	Work Timings					

IUH Cluster- Self Adequacy: (Individual capability to perform at work)

Your score: ___/24   (Low: 0-6 Average: 7-18
(fill it from scoring sheet)   High: 19-24)

Self-Adequacy:

Self-Adequacy indicates your ability to perform at work. It includes your nature being perfectionist/short-tempered overaggressive. It also includes your inadequate knowledge or skills of work.

Norms:

Social/Family - Gender and Age wise Norms (N=500, m=381 & f=119)						
Range	Low		Average		High	
Gender	Male	Female	Male	Female	Male	Female
Norms	7	6	8-11	7-12	12	13
Range	Low		Average		High	
Age	Greater than 35 years	Less than 35 years	Greater than 35 years	Less than 35 years	Greater than 35 years	Less than 35 years
Norms	6	6	7-10	7-11	11	12

Statement No	Sub Factor	Your Score (Shade the boxes)				
		0	1	2	3	4
Example: (if your score is 3)						
1	Skills					
2	Over Aggressive Nature					
3	Short tempered					
4	Nature					
5	Inadequate job knowledge					
6	Perfectionist					

SH Cluster- Openness: (Extent to which I can share my work life with my family members.)

Your score: ___/12   (Low: 0-3 Average: 4-9
(fill it from scoring sheet)   High: 10-12)

Openness:

Openness suggests extent to which you can share your work life with your family members. It not only includes family support but also sharing of problems and receiving guidance. Family culture plays a major role here.

Norms:

Social/Family - Gender and Age wise Norms (N=500, m=381 & f=119)						
Range	**Low**		**Average**		**High**	
Gender	Male	Female	Male	Female	Male	Female
Norms	6	7	7-8	8-9	9	10
Range	**Low**		**Average**		**High**	
Age	Greater than 35 years	Less than 35 years	Greater than 35 years	Less than 35 years	Greater than 35 years	Less than 35 years
Norms	5	6	6-8	7-9	9	10

Statement No	Sub Factor	Your Score (Shade the boxes)				
		0	1	2	3	4
Example: (if your score is 3)						
1	Support in Job					
2	Sharing problems & guidance					
3	Family culture					

SUH Cluster- Family Support: (Challenges faced from my immediate family that impacts my job.)

Your score: ___/24   (Low: 0-6 Average: 7-18
(fill it from scoring sheet)   High: 19-24)

Family Support:

Family support explains challenges faced by your family which affects your job. It includes nature of family members, financial insecurity, out stationed family, non-understanding family members and interpersonal relations with family members.

Norms:

Social/Family - Gender and Age wise Norms (N=500, m=381 & f=119)						
Range	**Low**		**Average**		**High**	
Gender	Male	Female	Male	Female	Male	Female
Norms	4	3	5-11	4-11	12	12
Range	**Low**		**Average**		**High**	
Age	Greater than 35 years	Less than 35 years	Greater than 35 years	Less than 35 years	Greater than 35 years	Less than 35 years
Norms	4	4	5-10	5-11	11	12

Statement No	Sub Factor	Your Score (Shade the boxes)				
		0	1	2	3	4
Example: (if your score is 3)						
1	Financial security					
2	Interpersonal relations in family					
3	Mobiles					
4	Family out stationed					
5	Not understanding					
6	Perfectionist					

OH Cluster- Employee Engagement: (The focus my company maintains in keeping its employees motivated and aligned.)

Your score: ___/20   (Low: 0-5 Average: 6-15
(fill it from scoring sheet)   High: 16-20)

Employee Engagement:

It indicates the focus your company's maintenance to keep employees motivated and aligned. It includes extra activities, motivation, encouragement, growth opportunities and responsibilities.

Norms:

Organizational - Gender and Age wise Norms (N=500, m=381 & f=119)					
Range	**Low**		**Average**		**High**	
Gender	Male	Female	Male	Female	Male	Female
Norms	11	11	11-14	12-14	15	15
Range	**Low**		**Average**		**High**	
Age	Greater than 35 years	Less than 35 years	Greater than 35 years	Less than 35 years	Greater than 35 years	Less than 35 years
Norms	11	11	12-13	12-14	14	15

Statement No	Sub Factor	Your Score (Shade the boxes)				
		0	1	2	3	4
Example: (if your score is 3)						
1	Extracurricular activities					
2	Responsibility					
3	Exposure					
4	Motivations					
5	Appreciation/ reward					

OUH Cluster- Organizational Support: (Organizational constraints that hinder Employee's performance.)

Your score: ___/12   (Low: 0-4 Average: 5-7
(fill it from scoring sheet)   High: 8-12)

Organizational support:

It indicates organizational constraints that hinder employee performance. It includes appreciation/reward, growth opportunities and transparency in work culture.

Norms:

Organizational - Gender and Age wise Norms (N=500, m=381 & f=119)						
Range	**Low**		**Average**		**High**	
Gender	**Male**	**Female**	**Male**	**Female**	**Male**	**Female**
Norms	4	4	5-7	5-7	8	9
Range	**Low**		**Average**		**High**	
Age	Greater than 35 years	Less than 35 years	Greater than 35 years	Less than 35 years	Greater than 35 years	Less than 35 years
Norms	4	5	5-7	6-7	8	9

Statement No	Sub Factor	Your Score (Shade the boxes)				
		0	**1**	**2**	**3**	**4**
Example: (if your score is 3)						
1	Appreciation/ reward					
2	Growth Opportunities					
3	Transparency					

Please Note: This is an abridged inventory, for full version please visit: www.choosehappiness.in

4

Application of Happiness Inventory

1. General Happiness Audit

Any organization is as happy as its employees and happy employees we have seen make an effective contribution at work place.

A general happiness audit of an organization or a department or an employee can be carried out.

The following steps are recommended:

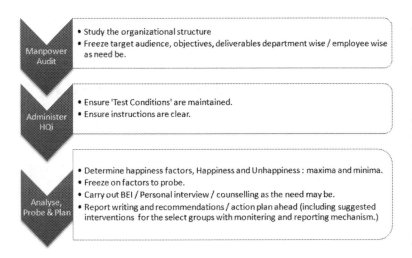

Manpower Audit
- Study the organizational structure
- Freeze target audience, objectives, deliverables department wise / employee wise as need be.

Administer HQi
- Ensure 'Test Conditions' are maintained.
- Ensure instructions are clear.

Analyse, Probe & Plan
- Determine happiness factors, Happiness and Unhappiness : maxima and minima.
- Freeze on factors to probe.
- Carry out BEI / Personal interview / counselling as the need may be.
- Report writing and recommendations / action plan ahead (including suggested interventions for the select groups with monitering and reporting mechanism.)

2. Happiness and Stress Audit

Along with the happiness audit, a stress audit can be carried out as under:

Phase I

Carrying out an exploration on stress tolerance limit (STL) with the help of psychometric instruments in terms of anxiety proneness, depression proneness, State/Trait Anger, & Type A Orientation, occupational Values, Dominant motive/need profile etc.

Phase II

Identifying the dominant organizational role stress dimensions. The main dimensions are as follows:

1. Inter-Role Distance (iRD)
2. Role Stagnation (RS)
3. Role Expectation Conflict (REC)
4. Role Erosion (RE)
5. Role Isolation (RI)
6. Personal Inadequacy (PI)
7. Self-Role Distance (SRD)
8. Role Ambiguity (RA)
9. Resource Inadequacy (RIN)
10. Role Overload (RO)

Phase III

Collecting the qualitative data on stress variables & their effects on individual health & performance by structured interview.

Phase IV

On the basis of the results obtained in above three phases, remedial measures are suggested to the organization for implementing suitable modification & changes in activities & practices in the organization.

This might also entail slight restructuring of the organization.

3. Other Applications of H.i.

- Career planning and counselling.
- Improve performance & productivity through personal effectiveness.
- Improve employee relations and employee engagement.
- Effective retention through improved level of job satisfaction.
- Cultivate 'Happy' Work culture Training needs identification.

5

Happy Ending

Lets summarize the 'happy learning':

- Happiness is a matter of choice. If you take the ownership to be happy, you will be happy and also spread happiness.
- Happiness at work place has 3 dimensions for an individual namely Individual, Family/social and Organizational. Each of these has 2 further sub dimension viz. Happy and Unhappy just like two sides of the same coin.
- Research has identified 164 factors that make us happy or unhappy at work place.
- Once the factors are identified, we know the reasons and thus can work on our action plan to be happy.
- Organizations struggle for happiness and productivity at work place but its not so difficult. The '**happy experiences**' shared in the book are real life example of how it can be achieved.
- If employees are constructively engaged and these factors are identified, it can help the organization create a happy work place leading to higher productivity.
- Individual at the same time need to gain insight into these factors, become aware of it and then take it one by one with acceptance as a path to happiness.
- Individuals, professionals and organizations can reach Dr. Yogesh Pahuja on Yogesh.pahuja@gmail.com or www.choosehappiness.in to join him in his pursuit to spread happiness.

Are you happy @ work?

Choose Happiness...Be Happy.

Notes/ References

- Bridget Murray (1998), Does 'emotional intelligence' matter in the workplace? APA monitor. Vol 29. No7.
- Diener, E. & Seligman, M.E.P. (2004), Beyond money: Toward and economy of well-being, Psychological Science in the Public Interest, Vol. 5, No. 1. pp 2-3; Watson, D., Pichler, F. and Wallace, C. (2010), Subjective Well-being in Europe, Second European Quality of Life Survey, European Foundation for the improvement of Living and Working condition.
- Dolan, P., Layard, R. & Metcalfe, R. (2011), Measuring subjective well-being for public policy, Office for National Statistics. Available at: http://www.statistics.gov.uk/articles/social_trends/measuring-subjective-wellbeing-for-public-policy.pdf;
- Fred Luthans, (2005), Organizational Behaviour. NY; McGraw hill.

- Fujiwara, D. & Campbell (2011), Valuation Techniques for Social Cost Benefit Analysis: Stated Preference, Revealed Preference and Subjective Well-being Approaches. HM Treasury. Available at: www.hm-treasury.gov.uk/d/green_book_valuationtechniques_250711.pdf.
- Hang Chang Chieh (1999), Nurturing Emotional Intelligence in University Students. APA monitor. Vol.2.No.1.
- Hicks, S. (2011), Spotlight on: Subjective Well-being, Office for National Statistics. Available at: http://www.statistics.gov.uk/articles/social_trends/spotlight-on-subjective-wellbeing.pdf.
- Huppert, F. et. al. (2009), Measuring Well-being Across Europe: Description of the ESS Well-being module and preliminary findings, Social Indicators Research, pp301-315; nef (2011), 'Measuring our progress', new economics foundation. Available at: http://www.neweconomics.org/publications/measuring-our-progress
- Marcela Kogan.(2001).Good things come in small packages. APA monitor vol32.january.issue no1
- Marcela Kogan(2001).where happiness lies. APA Monitor. vol 32. January. issue no.1
- Nissel, M. (1970), Social Trends, Vol. No. 1, Central Statistics Office, Her Majesty's Stationary Office.
- ONS (2012) (a), Initial findings from the consultation on proposed domains and measures of national well-being, Office for National Statistics. Available at: http://www.ons.gov.uk/ons/guide-method/user-guidance/well-being/publications/index.html
- ONS (2011) (b), Initial investigation into Subjective Well-being data from the ONS Opinions Survey, 1 December

2011, Office for National Statistics. Available at: http://www.ons.gov.uk/ons/guide-method/user-guidance/well being/publications/index.html

- ONS 2012(c), Analysis of experimental subjective well-being data from the Annual Population Survey, April - September 2011, 28 February 2012, Office for National Statistics. Available at: http://www.ons.gov.uk/ons/guide-method/user-guidance/well-being/publications/index.html

- Pahuja Yogesh (2012), Work culture and happiness: 'What makes employee happy at work place?'; Psyinsight March 2012, Volume 3, Issue no.1, 4-5.

- Pahuja Yogesh (2012), Understanding positive psychology and its relevance to organizations; Indian Journal of Positive Psychology June 2012, Volume 3, issue no.2, 189-190.

- Pareek. U. (2002), "Training instruments for HRD and OD", Tata McGraw-Hill, New Delhi, 2002

- Pestonjee, D. M. (1987), "Executive stress : Should it always be avoided?" Vikalpa, 12 (1), 23-30

- Pestonjee, D. M. (1989), "Stress and coping", Indira Gandhi National Open University, New Delhi.

- Pestonjee, D. M. (1991), "Stress and coping: the Indian experience", Sage Publications, New Delhi.

- Pestonjee, D. M. and Muncherji N. (1994), "Stress Audit: An HRD/OD Intervention", Indian Journal of Social Work, 2, 133-142

- Seligman, M.E.P., &Cs ikszentmihalyi, M. (2000). Positive Psychology: An introduction. American Psychologist, 55, 5-14

- Stiglitz-Sen-Fitoussi (2009), Report by the Commission on the Measurement of Economic Performance and Social Progress. Available at: www.stiglitzsenfitoussi.fr/documents/rapport_anglais.pdf